THE ROAD NOT TAKEN AND SELECTED POEMS

by

ROBERT FROST

COMPASS CIRCLE

Note:
All efforts have been made to preserve original spellings and punctuation of the original edition which may include old-fashioned English spellings of words and archaic variants.

This book is a product of its time and does not reflect the same views on race, gen-der, sexuality, ethnicity, and interpersonal relations as it would if it were written today.

For information contact :
information@compass-circle.com

Never be bullied into silence. Never allow yourself to be made a victim. Accept no one's definition of your life; define yourself.

ROBERT FROST

SECRET WISDOM OF THE AGES SERIES

Life presents itself, it advances in a fast way. Life indeed never stops. It never stops until the end. The most diverse questions peek and fade in our minds. Sometimes we seek for answers. Sometimes we just let time go by.

The book you have now in your hands has been waiting to be discovered by you. This book may reveal the answers to some of your questions.

Books are friends. Friends who are always by your side and who can give you great ideas, advice or just comfort your soul.

A great book can make you see things in your soul that you have not yet discovered, make you see things in your soul that you were not aware of.

Great books can change your life for the better. They can make you understand fascinating theories, give you new ideas, inspire you to undertake new challenges or to walk along new paths.

Life philosophies like the one of Robert Frost are indeed a secret to many, but for those of us lucky enough to have discovered them, by one way or another, these books can enlighten us. They can open a wide range of possibilities to us. Because achieving greatness requires knowledge.

The series SECRET WISDOM OF THE AGES presented by Compass Circle try to bring you the great timeless masterpieces of personal development, positive thinking, and the law of attraction.

We welcome you to discover with us fascinating works by William Blake, Socrates, Plato, Henry Thoreau, among others.

Contents

III A BOY'S WILL 69

Part I

SELECTED POEMS

1

FIRE AND ICE

Some say the world will end in fire,
   Some say in ice.
From what I've tasted of desire
I hold with those who favor fire.
But if it had to perish twice,
I think I know enough of hate
To know that for destruction ice
Is also great,
And would suffice.

2

THE GRINDSTONE

Having a wheel and four legs of its own
   Has never availed the cumbersome grindstone
   To get it anywhere that I can see.
   These hands have helped it go and even race;
   Not all the motion, though, they ever lent,
   Not all the miles it may have thought it went,
   Have got it one step from the starting place.
   It stands beside the same old apple tree.
   The shadow of the apple tree is thin
   Upon it now; its feet are fast in snow.
   All other farm machinery's gone in,
   And some of it on no more legs and wheel

2

Than the grindstone can boast to stand or go.
(I'm thinking chiefly of the wheelbarrow.)
For months it hasn't known the taste of steel,
Washed down with rusty water in a tin.
But standing outdoors, hungry, in the cold,
Except in towns, at night, is not a sin.
And, anyway, its standing in the yard
Under a ruinous live apple tree
Has nothing any more to do with me,
Except that I remember how of old,
One summer day, all day I drove it hard,
And some one mounted on it rode it hard,
And he and I between us ground a blade.

I gave it the preliminary spin,
And poured on water (tears it might have been);
And when it almost gayly jumped and flowed,
A Father-Time-like man got on and rode,
Armed with a scythe and spectacles that glowed.
He turned on will-power to increase the load
And slow me down—and I abruptly slowed,
Like coming to a sudden railroad station.
I changed from hand to hand in desperation.

I wondered what machine of ages gone
This represented an improvement on.
For all I knew it may have sharpened spears
And arrowheads itself. Much use for years
Had gradually worn it an oblate
Spheroid that kicked and struggled in its gait,
Appearing to return me hate for hate.
(But I forgive it now as easily
As any other boyhood enemy

3

Whose pride has failed to get him anywhere.)
I wondered who it was the man thought ground–
The one who held the wheel back or the one
Who gave his life to keep it going round?
I wondered if he really thought it fair
For him to have the say when we were done.
Such were the bitter thoughts to which I turned.

Not for myself was I so much concerned.
Oh, no!–although, of course, I could have found
A better way to pass the afternoon
Than grinding discord out of a grindstone,
And beating insects at their gritty tune.
Nor was I for the man so much concerned.
Once when the grindstone almost jumped its bearing
It looked as if he might be badly thrown
And wounded on his blade. So far from caring,
I laughed inside, and only cranked the faster,
(It ran as if it wasn't greased but glued);
I welcomed any moderate disaster
That might be calculated to postpone
What evidently nothing could conclude.

The thing that made me more and more afraid
Was that we'd ground it sharp and hadn't known,
And now were only wasting precious blade.
And when he raised it dripping once and tried
The creepy edge of it with wary touch,
And viewed it over his glasses funny-eyed,
Only disinterestedly to decide
It needed a turn more, I could have cried
Wasn't there danger of a turn too much?
Mightn't we make it worse instead of better?

I was for leaving something to the whetter.
What if it wasn't all it should be? I'd
Be satisfied if he'd be satisfied.

3

A BROOK IN THE CITY

The farm house lingers, though averse to square
  With the new city street it has to wear
  A number in. But what about the brook
  That held the house as in an elbow-crook?
  I ask as one who knew the brook, its strength
  And impulse, having dipped a finger-length
  And made it leap my knuckle, having tossed
  A flower to try its currents where they crossed.
  The meadow grass could be cemented down
  From growing under pavements of a town;
  The apple trees be sent to hearth-stone flame.
  Is water wood to serve a brook the same?
  How else dispose of an immortal force
  No longer needed? Staunch it at its source
  With cinder loads dumped down? The brook was thrown
  Deep in a sewer dungeon under stone
  In fetid darkness still to live and run—
  And all for nothing it had ever done
  Except forget to go in fear perhaps.
  No one would know except for ancient maps
  That such a brook ran water. But I wonder
  If, from its being kept forever under,
  These thoughts may not have risen that so keep

This new-built city from both work and sleep.

4

DESIGN

I found a dimpled spider, fat and white,
  On a white heal-all, holding up a moth
  Like a white piece of rigid satin cloth–
  Assorted characters of death and blight
  Mixed ready to begin the morning right,
  Like the ingredients of a witches' broth–
  A snow-drop spider, a flower like froth,
  And dead wings carried like a paper kite.

What had that flower to do with being white,
  The wayside blue and innocent heal-all?
  What brought the kindred spider to that height,
  Then steered the white moth thither in the night?
  What but design of darkness to appal?–
  If design govern in a thing so small.

Part II

MOUNTAIN INTERVAL

1

THE ROAD NOT TAKEN

Two roads diverged in a yellow wood,
And sorry I could not travel both
And be one traveler, long I stood
And looked down one as far as I could
To where it bent in the undergrowth;

Then took the other, as just as fair,
And having perhaps the better claim,
Because it was grassy and wanted wear;
Though as for that the passing there
Had worn them really about the same,

And both that morning equally lay
In leaves no step had trodden black.
Oh, I kept the first for another day!
Yet knowing how way leads on to way,
I doubted if I should ever come back.

I shall be telling this with a sigh
Somewhere ages and ages hence:
Two roads diverged in a wood, and I–
I took the one less traveled by,
And that has made all the difference.

2

CHRISTMAS TREES

(A Christmas Circular Letter)

The city had withdrawn into itself
And left at last the country to the country;
When between whirls of snow not come to lie
And whirls of foliage not yet laid, there drove
A stranger to our yard, who looked the city,
Yet did in country fashion in that there
He sat and waited till he drew us out
A-buttoning coats to ask him who he was.
He proved to be the city come again
To look for something it had left behind
And could not do without and keep its Christmas.
He asked if I would sell my Christmas trees;
My woods–the young fir balsams like a place
Where houses all are churches and have spires.
I hadn't thought of them as Christmas Trees.
I doubt if I was tempted for a moment
To sell them off their feet to go in cars
And leave the slope behind the house all bare,
Where the sun shines now no warmer than the moon.
I'd hate to have them know it if I was.
Yet more I'd hate to hold my trees except
As others hold theirs or refuse for them,
Beyond the time of profitable growth,
The trial by market everything must come to.
I dallied so much with the thought of selling.
Then whether from mistaken courtesy

And fear of seeming short of speech, or whether
From hope of hearing good of what was mine,
I said, "There aren't enough to be worth while."
"I could soon tell how many they would cut,
You let me look them over."

"You could look.
But don't expect I'm going to let you have them."
Pasture they spring in, some in clumps too close
That lop each other of boughs, but not a few
Quite solitary and having equal boughs
All round and round. The latter he nodded "Yes" to,
Or paused to say beneath some lovelier one,
With a buyer's moderation, "That would do."
I thought so too, but wasn't there to say so.
We climbed the pasture on the south, crossed over,
And came down on the north.

He said, "A thousand."

"A thousand Christmas trees!—at what apiece?"

He felt some need of softening that to me:
"A thousand trees would come to thirty dollars."

Then I was certain I had never meant
To let him have them. Never show surprise!
But thirty dollars seemed so small beside
The extent of pasture I should strip, three cents
(For that was all they figured out apiece),
Three cents so small beside the dollar friends
I should be writing to within the hour
Would pay in cities for good trees like those,

Regular vestry-trees whole Sunday Schools
Could hang enough on to pick off enough.
A thousand Christmas trees I didn't know I had!
Worth three cents more to give away than sell,
As may be shown by a simple calculation.
Too bad I couldn't lay one in a letter.
I can't help wishing I could send you one,
In wishing you herewith a Merry Christmas.

3

AN OLD MAN'S WINTER NIGHT

All out of doors looked darkly in at him
 Through the thin frost, almost in separate stars,
That gathers on the pane in empty rooms.
What kept his eyes from giving back the gaze
Was the lamp tilted near them in his hand.
What kept him from remembering what it was
That brought him to that creaking room was age.
He stood with barrels round him—at a loss.
And having scared the cellar under him
In clomping there, he scared it once again
In clomping off;—and scared the outer night,
Which has its sounds, familiar, like the roar
Of trees and crack of branches, common things,
But nothing so like beating on a box.
A light he was to no one but himself
Where now he sat, concerned with he knew what,
A quiet light, and then not even that.
He consigned to the moon, such as she was,

So late-arising, to the broken moon
As better than the sun in any case
For such a charge, his snow upon the roof,
His icicles along the wall to keep;
And slept. The log that shifted with a jolt
Once in the stove, disturbed him and he shifted,
And eased his heavy breathing, but still slept.
One aged man–one man–can't fill a house,
A farm, a countryside, or if he can,
It's thus he does it of a winter night.

4

A PATCH OF OLD SNOW

There's a patch of old snow in a corner
　　That I should have guessed
Was a blow-away paper the rain
　　Had brought to rest.

It is speckled with grime as if
　　Small print overspread it,
The news of a day I've forgotten–
　　If I ever read it.

5

IN THE HOME STRETCH

She stood against the kitchen sink, and looked
   Over the sink out through a dusty window
   At weeds the water from the sink made tall.
   She wore her cape; her hat was in her hand.
   Behind her was confusion in the room,
   Of chairs turned upside down to sit like people
   In other chairs, and something, come to look,
   For every room a house has—parlor, bed-room,
   And dining-room—thrown pell-mell in the kitchen.
   And now and then a smudged, infernal face
   Looked in a door behind her and addressed
   Her back. She always answered without turning.

"Where will I put this walnut bureau, lady?"
"Put it on top of something that's on top
   Of something else," she laughed. "Oh, put it where
   You can to-night, and go. It's almost dark;
   You must be getting started back to town."
   Another blackened face thrust in and looked
   And smiled, and when she did not turn, spoke gently,
"What are you seeing out the window, *lady*?"

"Never was I beladied so before.
   Would evidence of having been called lady
   More than so many times make me a lady
   In common law, I wonder."

"But I ask,

What are you seeing out the window, lady?"

"What I'll be seeing more of in the years
To come as here I stand and go the round
Of many plates with towels many times."

"And what is that? You only put me off."

"Rank weeds that love the water from the dish-pan
More than some women like the dish-pan, Joe;
A little stretch of mowing-field for you;
Not much of that until I come to woods
That end all. And it's scarce enough to call
A view."

"And yet you think you like it, dear?"

"That's what you're so concerned to know! You hope
I like it. Bang goes something big away
Off there upstairs. The very tread of men
As great as those is shattering to the frame
Of such a little house. Once left alone,
You and I, dear, will go with softer steps
Up and down stairs and through the rooms, and none
But sudden winds that snatch them from our hands
Will ever slam the doors."

"I think you see

More than you like to own to out that window."

"No; for besides the things I tell you of,
I only see the years. They come and go
In alternation with the weeds, the field,
The wood."

"What kind of years?"

"Why, latter years—

Different from early years."

"I see them, too.

You didn't count them?"

"No, the further off

So ran together that I didn't try to.
It can scarce be that they would be in number
We'd care to know, for we are not young now.
And bang goes something else away off there.
It sounds as if it were the men went down,
And every crash meant one less to return
To lighted city streets we, too, have known,
But now are giving up for country darkness."

"Come from that window where you see too much for me,
And take a livelier view of things from here.
They're going. Watch this husky swarming up
Over the wheel into the sky-high seat,
Lighting his pipe now, squinting down his nose
At the flame burning downward as he sucks it."

"See how it makes his nose-side bright, a proof
How dark it's getting. Can you tell what time
It is by that? Or by the moon? The new moon!
What shoulder did I see her over? Neither.
A wire she is of silver, as new as we
To everything. Her light won't last us long.
It's something, though, to know we're going to have her
Night after night and stronger every night
To see us through our first two weeks. But, Joe,
The stove! Before they go! Knock on the window;
Ask them to help you get it on its feet.
We stand here dreaming. Hurry! Call them back!"

"They're not gone yet."

"We've got to have the stove,

Whatever else we want for. And a light.
Have we a piece of candle if the lamp
And oil are buried out of reach?"

Again

The house was full of tramping, and the dark,
Door-filling men burst in and seized the stove.
A cannon-mouth-like hole was in the wall,
To which they set it true by eye; and then
Came up the jointed stovepipe in their hands,
So much too light and airy for their strength
It almost seemed to come ballooning up,
Slipping from clumsy clutches toward the ceiling.
"A fit!" said one, and banged a stovepipe shoulder.
"It's good luck when you move in to begin

16

With good luck with your stovepipe. Never mind,
It's not so bad in the country, settled down,
When people're getting on in life. You'll like it."
Joe said: "You big boys ought to find a farm,
And make good farmers, and leave other fellows
The city work to do. There's not enough
For everybody as it is in there."
"God!" one said wildly, and, when no one spoke:
"Say that to Jimmy here. He needs a farm."
But Jimmy only made his jaw recede
Fool-like, and rolled his eyes as if to say
He saw himself a farmer. Then there was a French boy
Who said with seriousness that made them laugh,
"Ma friend, you ain't know what it is you're ask."
He doffed his cap and held it with both hands
Across his chest to make as 'twere a bow:
"We're giving you our chances on de farm."
And then they all turned to with deafening boots
And put each other bodily out of the house.
"Goodby to them! We puzzle them. They think–
I don't know what they think we see in what
They leave us to: that pasture slope that seems
The back some farm presents us; and your woods
To northward from your window at the sink,
Waiting to steal a step on us whenever
We drop our eyes or turn to other things,
As in the game 'Ten-step' the children play."

"Good boys they seemed, and let them love the city.
All they could say was 'God!' when you proposed
Their coming out and making useful farmers."

"Did they make something lonesome go through you?

17

It would take more than them to sicken you—
Us of our bargain. But they left us so
As to our fate, like fools past reasoning with.
They almost shook *me*."

"It's all so much

What we have always wanted, I confess
It's seeming bad for a moment makes it seem
Even worse still, and so on down, down, down.
It's nothing; it's their leaving us at dusk.
I never bore it well when people went.
The first night after guests have gone, the house
Seems haunted or exposed. I always take
A personal interest in the locking up
At bedtime; but the strangeness soon wears off."
He fetched a dingy lantern from behind
A door. "There's that we didn't lose! And these!"—
Some matches he unpocketed. "For food—
The meals we've had no one can take from us.
I wish that everything on earth were just
As certain as the meals we've had. I wish
The meals we haven't had were, anyway.
What have you you know where to lay your hands on?"

"The bread we bought in passing at the store.
There's butter somewhere, too."

"Let's rend the bread.
I'll light the fire for company for you;
You'll not have any other company
Till Ed begins to get out on a Sunday
To look us over and give us his idea

Of what wants pruning, shingling, breaking up.
He'll know what he would do if he were we,
And all at once. He'll plan for us and plan
To help us, but he'll take it out in planning.
Well, you can set the table with the loaf.
Let's see you find your loaf. I'll light the fire.
I like chairs occupying other chairs
Not offering a lady–"

"There again, Joe!

You're tired."

"I'm drunk-nonsensical tired out;

Don't mind a word I say. It's a day's work
To empty one house of all household goods
And fill another with 'em fifteen miles away,
Although you do no more than dump them down."

"Dumped down in paradise we are and happy."

"It's all so much what I have always wanted,
I can't believe it's what you wanted, too."

"Shouldn't you like to know?"

"I'd like to know

If it is what you wanted, then how much
You wanted it for me."

"A troubled conscience!

You don't want me to tell if *I* don't know."

"I don't want to find out what can't be known.

But who first said the word to come?"

"My dear,

It's who first thought the thought. You're searching, Joe,
For things that don't exist; I mean beginnings.
Ends and beginnings–there are no such things.
There are only middles."

"What is this?"

"This life?

Our sitting here by lantern-light together
Amid the wreckage of a former home?
You won't deny the lantern isn't new.
The stove is not, and you are not to me,
Nor I to you."

"Perhaps you never were?"

"It would take me forever to recite
All that's not new in where we find ourselves.
New is a word for fools in towns who think
Style upon style in dress and thought at last
Must get somewhere. I've heard you say as much.

No, this is no beginning."

"Then an end?"

"End is a gloomy word."

"Is it too late

To drag you out for just a good-night call
On the old peach trees on the knoll to grope
By starlight in the grass for a last peach
The neighbors may not have taken as their right
When the house wasn't lived in? I've been looking:
I doubt if they have left us many grapes.
Before we set ourselves to right the house,
The first thing in the morning, out we go
To go the round of apple, cherry, peach,
Pine, alder, pasture, mowing, well, and brook.
All of a farm it is."

"I know this much:

I'm going to put you in your bed, if first
I have to make you build it. Come, the light."

When there was no more lantern in the kitchen,
The fire got out through crannies in the stove
And danced in yellow wrigglers on the ceiling,
As much at home as if they'd always danced there.

6

THE TELEPHONE

"When I was just as far as I could walk
    From here to-day,
    There was an hour
    All still
    When leaning with my head against a flower
    I heard you talk.
    Don't say I didn't, for I heard you say—
    You spoke from that flower on the window sill—
    Do you remember what it was you said?"

"First tell me what it was you thought you heard."

"Having found the flower and driven a bee away,
    I leaned my head,
    And holding by the stalk,
    I listened and I thought I caught the word—
    What was it? Did you call me by my name?
    Or did you say—
    Someone said 'Come'—I heard it as I bowed."

"I may have thought as much, but not aloud."

"Well, so I came."

7

MEETING AND PASSING

As I went down the hill along the wall
    There was a gate I had leaned at for the view
    And had just turned from when I first saw you
    As you came up the hill. We met. But all
    We did that day was mingle great and small
    Footprints in summer dust as if we drew
    The figure of our being less than two
    But more than one as yet. Your parasol

    Pointed the decimal off with one deep thrust.
    And all the time we talked you seemed to see
    Something down there to smile at in the dust.
    (Oh, it was without prejudice to me!)
    Afterward I went past what you had passed
    Before we met and you what I had passed.

8

HYLA BROOK

By June our brook's run out of song and speed.
    Sought for much after that, it will be found
    Either to have gone groping underground
    (And taken with it all the Hyla breed
    That shouted in the mist a month ago,
    Like ghost of sleigh-bells in a ghost of snow)–

Or flourished and come up in jewel-weed,
Weak foliage that is blown upon and bent
Even against the way its waters went.
Its bed is left a faded paper sheet
Of dead leaves stuck together by the heat–
A brook to none but who remember long.
This as it will be seen is other far
Than with brooks taken otherwhere in song.
We love the things we love for what they are.

9

THE OVEN BIRD

There is a singer everyone has heard,
    Loud, a mid-summer and a mid-wood bird,
    Who makes the solid tree trunks sound again.
    He says that leaves are old and that for flowers
    Mid-summer is to spring as one to ten.
    He says the early petal-fall is past
    When pear and cherry bloom went down in showers
    On sunny days a moment overcast;
    And comes that other fall we name the fall.
    He says the highway dust is over all.
    The bird would cease and be as other birds
    But that he knows in singing not to sing.
    The question that he frames in all but words
    Is what to make of a diminished thing.

10

BOND AND FREE

Love has earth to which she clings
   With hills and circling arms about–
   Wall within wall to shut fear out.
   But Thought has need of no such things,
   For Thought has a pair of dauntless wings.

   On snow and sand and turf, I see
   Where Love has left a printed trace
   With straining in the world's embrace.
   And such is Love and glad to be.
   But Thought has shaken his ankles free.

   Thought cleaves the interstellar gloom
   And sits in Sirius' disc all night,
   Till day makes him retrace his flight,
   With smell of burning on every plume,
   Back past the sun to an earthly room.

   His gains in heaven are what they are.
   Yet some say Love by being thrall
   And simply staying possesses all
   In several beauty that Thought fares far
   To find fused in another star.

11

BIRCHES

When I see birches bend to left and right
  Across the lines of straighter darker trees,
  I like to think some boy's been swinging them.
  But swinging doesn't bend them down to stay.
  Ice-storms do that. Often you must have seen them
  Loaded with ice a sunny winter morning
  After a rain. They click upon themselves
  As the breeze rises, and turn many-colored
  As the stir cracks and crazes their enamel.
  Soon the sun's warmth makes them shed crystal shells
  Shattering and avalanching on the snow-crust–
  Such heaps of broken glass to sweep away
  You'd think the inner dome of heaven had fallen.
  They are dragged to the withered bracken by the load,
  And they seem not to break; though once they are bowed
  So low for long, they never right themselves:
  You may see their trunks arching in the woods
  Years afterwards, trailing their leaves on the ground
  Like girls on hands and knees that throw their hair
  Before them over their heads to dry in the sun.
  But I was going to say when Truth broke in
  With all her matter-of-fact about the ice-storm
  (Now am I free to be poetical?)
  I should prefer to have some boy bend them
  As he went out and in to fetch the cows–
  Some boy too far from town to learn baseball,
  Whose only play was what he found himself,

Summer or winter, and could play alone.
One by one he subdued his father's trees
By riding them down over and over again
Until he took the stiffness out of them,
And not one but hung limp, not one was left
For him to conquer. He learned all there was
To learn about not launching out too soon
And so not carrying the tree away
Clear to the ground. He always kept his poise
To the top branches, climbing carefully
With the same pains you use to fill a cup
Up to the brim, and even above the brim.
Then he flung outward, feet first, with a swish,
Kicking his way down through the air to the ground.
So was I once myself a swinger of birches.
And so I dream of going back to be.
It's when I'm weary of considerations,
And life is too much like a pathless wood
Where your face burns and tickles with the cobwebs
Broken across it, and one eye is weeping
From a twig's having lashed across it open.
I'd like to get away from earth awhile
And then come back to it and begin over.
May no fate willfully misunderstand me
And half grant what I wish and snatch me away
Not to return. Earth's the right place for love:
I don't know where it's likely to go better.
I'd like to go by climbing a birch tree,
And climb black branches up a snow-white trunk
Toward heaven, till the tree could bear no more,
But dipped its top and set me down again.
That would be good both going and coming back.
One could do worse than be a swinger of birches.

12

PEA BRUSH

I walked down alone Sunday after church
    To the place where John has been cutting trees
    To see for myself about the birch
    He said I could have to bush my peas.

    The sun in the new-cut narrow gap
    Was hot enough for the first of May,
    And stifling hot with the odor of sap
    From stumps still bleeding their life away.

    The frogs that were peeping a thousand shrill
    Wherever the ground was low and wet,
    The minute they heard my step went still
    To watch me and see what I came to get.

    Birch boughs enough piled everywhere!–
    All fresh and sound from the recent axe.
    Time someone came with cart and pair
    And got them off the wild flower's backs.

    They might be good for garden things
    To curl a little finger round,
    The same as you seize cat's-cradle strings,
    And lift themselves up off the ground.

    Small good to anything growing wild,
    They were crooking many a trillium

That had budded before the boughs were piled
And since it was coming up had to come.

13

PUTTING IN THE SEED

You come to fetch me from my work to-night
    When supper's on the table, and we'll see
    If I can leave off burying the white
    Soft petals fallen from the apple tree.
    (Soft petals, yes, but not so barren quite,
    Mingled with these, smooth bean and wrinkled pea;)
    And go along with you ere you lose sight
    Of what you came for and become like me,
    Slave to a springtime passion for the earth.
    How Love burns through the Putting in the Seed
    On through the watching for that early birth
    When, just as the soil tarnishes with weed,

    The sturdy seedling with arched body comes
    Shouldering its way and shedding the earth crumbs.

14

A TIME TO TALK

When a friend calls to me from the road
   And slows his horse to a meaning walk,
   I don't stand still and look around
On all the hills I haven't hoed,
   And shout from where I am, What is it?
No, not as there is a time to talk.
   I thrust my hoe in the mellow ground,
   Blade-end up and five feet tall,
   And plod: I go up to the stone wall
For a friendly visit.

15

THE COW IN APPLE TIME

Something inspires the only cow of late
   To make no more of a wall than an open gate,
   And think no more of wall-builders than fools.
   Her face is flecked with pomace and she drools
A cider syrup. Having tasted fruit,
   She scorns a pasture withering to the root.
   She runs from tree to tree where lie and sweeten
The windfalls spiked with stubble and worm-eaten.
   She leaves them bitten when she has to fly.
   She bellows on a knoll against the sky.
   Her udder shrivels and the milk goes dry.

16

AN ENCOUNTER

Once on the kind of day called "weather breeder,"
    When the heat slowly hazes and the sun
    By its own power seems to be undone,
    I was half boring through, half climbing through
    A swamp of cedar. Choked with oil of cedar
    And scurf of plants, and weary and over-heated,
    And sorry I ever left the road I knew,
    I paused and rested on a sort of hook
    That had me by the coat as good as seated,
    And since there was no other way to look,
    Looked up toward heaven, and there against the blue,
    Stood over me a resurrected tree,
    A tree that had been down and raised again–
    A barkless spectre. He had halted too,
    As if for fear of treading upon me.
    I saw the strange position of his hands–
    Up at his shoulders, dragging yellow strands
    Of wire with something in it from men to men.
    "You here?" I said. "Where aren't you nowadays
    And what's the news you carry–if you know?
    And tell me where you're off for–Montreal?
    Me? I'm not off for anywhere at all.
    Sometimes I wander out of beaten ways
    Half looking for the orchid Calypso."

17

RANGE-FINDING

The battle rent a cobweb diamond-strung
    And cut a flower beside a ground bird's nest
    Before it stained a single human breast.
    The stricken flower bent double and so hung.
    And still the bird revisited her young.
    A butterfly its fall had dispossessed
    A moment sought in air his flower of rest,
    Then lightly stooped to it and fluttering clung.

On the bare upland pasture there had spread
    O'ernight 'twixt mullein stalks a wheel of thread
    And straining cables wet with silver dew.
    A sudden passing bullet shook it dry.
    The indwelling spider ran to greet the fly,
    But finding nothing, sullenly withdrew.

18

THE HILL WIFE

LONELINESS

(Her Word)

One ought not to have to care
So much as you and I
Care when the birds come round the house
To seem to say good-bye;

Or care so much when they come back
With whatever it is they sing;
The truth being we are as much
Too glad for the one thing

As we are too sad for the other here—
With birds that fill their breasts
But with each other and themselves
And their built or driven nests.

HOUSE FEAR

Always—I tell you this they learned—
    Always at night when they returned
To the lonely house from far away
To lamps unlighted and fire gone gray,
They learned to rattle the lock and key
To give whatever might chance to be
Warning and time to be off in flight:
And preferring the out- to the in-door night,

They learned to leave the house-door wide
Until they had lit the lamp inside.

THE SMILE

(*Her Word*)

I didn't like the way he went away.
That smile! It never came of being gay.
Still he smiled–did you see him?–I was sure!
Perhaps because we gave him only bread
And the wretch knew from that that we were poor.
Perhaps because he let us give instead
Of seizing from us as he might have seized.
Perhaps he mocked at us for being wed,
Or being very young (and he was pleased
To have a vision of us old and dead).
I wonder how far down the road he's got.
He's watching from the woods as like as not.

THE OFT-REPEATED DREAM

She had no saying dark enough
    For the dark pine that kept
    Forever trying the window-latch
    Of the room where they slept.

    The tireless but ineffectual hands
    That with every futile pass
    Made the great tree seem as a little bird
    Before the mystery of glass!

    It never had been inside the room,
    And only one of the two

Was afraid in an oft-repeated dream
Of what the tree might do.

THE IMPULSE

It was too lonely for her there,
    And too wild,
And since there were but two of them,
    And no child,

And work was little in the house,
    She was free,
And followed where he furrowed field,
    Or felled tree.

She rested on a log and tossed
    The fresh chips,
With a song only to herself
    On her lips.

And once she went to break a bough
    Of black alder.
She strayed so far she scarcely heard
    When he called her–

And didn't answer–didn't speak–
    Or return.
She stood, and then she ran and hid
    In the fern.

He never found her, though he looked
    Everywhere,
And he asked at her mother's house

Was she there.

Sudden and swift and light as that
The ties gave,
And he learned of finalities
Besides the grave.

19

THE BONFIRE

"Oh, let's go up the hill and scare ourselves,
　　As reckless as the best of them to-night,
　　By setting fire to all the brush we piled
　　With pitchy hands to wait for rain or snow.
　　Oh, let's not wait for rain to make it safe.
　　The pile is ours: we dragged it bough on bough
　　Down dark converging paths between the pines.
　　Let's not care what we do with it to-night.
　　Divide it? No! But burn it as one pile
　　The way we piled it. And let's be the talk
　　Of people brought to windows by a light
　　Thrown from somewhere against their wall-paper.
　　Rouse them all, both the free and not so free
　　With saying what they'd like to do to us
　　For what they'd better wait till we have done.
　　Let's all but bring to life this old volcano,
　　If that is what the mountain ever was–
　　And scare ourselves. Let wild fire loose we will...."

"And scare you too?" the children said together.

"Why wouldn't it scare me to have a fire
Begin in smudge with ropy smoke and know
That still, if I repent, I may recall it,
But in a moment not: a little spurt
Of burning fatness, and then nothing but
The fire itself can put it out, and that
By burning out, and before it burns out
It will have roared first and mixed sparks with stars,
And sweeping round it with a flaming sword,
Made the dim trees stand back in wider circle—
Done so much and I know not how much more
I mean it shall not do if I can bind it.
Well if it doesn't with its draft bring on
A wind to blow in earnest from some quarter,
As once it did with me upon an April.
The breezes were so spent with winter blowing
They seemed to fail the bluebirds under them
Short of the perch their languid flight was toward;
And my flame made a pinnacle to heaven
As I walked once round it in possession.
But the wind out of doors—you know the saying.
There came a gust. You used to think the trees
Made wind by fanning since you never knew
It blow but that you saw the trees in motion.
Something or someone watching made that gust.
It put the flame tip-down and dabbed the grass
Of over-winter with the least tip-touch
Your tongue gives salt or sugar in your hand.
The place it reached to blackened instantly.
The black was all there was by day-light,
That and the merest curl of cigarette smoke—

37

And a flame slender as the hepaticas,
Blood-root, and violets so soon to be now.
But the black spread like black death on the ground,
And I think the sky darkened with a cloud
Like winter and evening coming on together.
There were enough things to be thought of then.
Where the field stretches toward the north
And setting sun to Hyla brook, I gave it
To flames without twice thinking, where it verges
Upon the road, to flames too, though in fear
They might find fuel there, in withered brake,
Grass its full length, old silver golden-rod,
And alder and grape vine entanglement,
To leap the dusty deadline. For my own
I took what front there was beside. I knelt
And thrust hands in and held my face away.
Fight such a fire by rubbing not by beating.
A board is the best weapon if you have it.
I had my coat. And oh, I knew, I knew,
And said out loud, I couldn't bide the smother
And heat so close in; but the thought of all
The woods and town on fire by me, and all
The town turned out to fight for me—that held me.
I trusted the brook barrier, but feared
The road would fail; and on that side the fire
Died not without a noise of crackling wood—
Of something more than tinder-grass and weed—
That brought me to my feet to hold it back
By leaning back myself, as if the reins
Were round my neck and I was at the plough.
I won! But I'm sure no one ever spread
Another color over a tenth the space
That I spread coal-black over in the time

It took me. Neighbors coming home from town
Couldn't believe that so much black had come there
While they had backs turned, that it hadn't been there
When they had passed an hour or so before
Going the other way and they not seen it.
They looked about for someone to have done it.
But there was no one. I was somewhere wondering
Where all my weariness had gone and why
I walked so light on air in heavy shoes
In spite of a scorched Fourth-of-July feeling.
Why wouldn't I be scared remembering that?"

"If it scares you, what will it do to us?"

"Scare you. But if you shrink from being scared,
What would you say to war if it should come?
That's what for reasons I should like to know—
If you can comfort me by any answer."

"Oh, but war's not for children—it's for men."

"Now we are digging almost down to China.
My dears, my dears, you thought that—we all thought it.
So your mistake was ours. Haven't you heard, though,
About the ships where war has found them out
At sea, about the towns where war has come
Through opening clouds at night with droning speed
Further o'erhead than all but stars and angels,—
And children in the ships and in the towns?
Haven't you heard what we have lived to learn?
Nothing so new—something we had forgotten:
War is for everyone, for children too.
I wasn't going to tell you and I mustn't.

The best way is to come up hill with me
And have our fire and laugh and be afraid."

20

A GIRL'S GARDEN

A neighbor of mine in the village
    Likes to tell how one spring
    When she was a girl on the farm, she did
    A childlike thing.

    One day she asked her father
    To give her a garden plot
    To plant and tend and reap herself,
    And he said, "Why not?"

    In casting about for a corner
    He thought of an idle bit
    Of walled-off ground where a shop had stood,
    And he said, "Just it."

    And he said, "That ought to make you
    An ideal one-girl farm,
    And give you a chance to put some strength
    On your slim-jim arm."

    It was not enough of a garden,
    Her father said, to plough;
    So she had to work it all by hand,

But she don't mind now.

She wheeled the dung in the wheelbarrow
Along a stretch of road;
But she always ran away and left
Her not-nice load.

And hid from anyone passing.
And then she begged the seed.
She says she thinks she planted one
Of all things but weed.

A hill each of potatoes,
Radishes, lettuce, peas,
Tomatoes, beets, beans, pumpkins, corn,
And even fruit trees.

And yes, she has long mistrusted
That a cider apple tree
In bearing there to-day is hers,
Or at least may be.

Her crop was a miscellany
When all was said and done,
A little bit of everything,
A great deal of none.

Now when she sees in the village
How village things go,
Just when it seems to come in right,
She says, "*I* know!

It's as when I was a farmer——"

Oh, never by way of advice!
And she never sins by telling the tale
To the same person twice.

21

THE EXPOSED NEST

You were forever finding some new play.
    So when I saw you down on hands and knees
In the meadow, busy with the new-cut hay,
Trying, I thought, to set it up on end,
I went to show you how to make it stay,
If that was your idea, against the breeze,
And, if you asked me, even help pretend
To make it root again and grow afresh.
But 'twas no make-believe with you to-day,
Nor was the grass itself your real concern,
Though I found your hand full of wilted fern,
Steel-bright June-grass, and blackening heads of clover.
'Twas a nest full of young birds on the ground
The cutter-bar had just gone champing over
(Miraculously without tasting flesh)
And left defenseless to the heat and light.
You wanted to restore them to their right
Of something interposed between their sight
And too much world at once—could means be found.
The way the nest-full every time we stirred
Stood up to us as to a mother-bird
Whose coming home has been too long deferred,
Made me ask would the mother-bird return

42

And care for them in such a change of scene
And might our meddling make her more afraid.
That was a thing we could not wait to learn.
We saw the risk we took in doing good,
But dared not spare to do the best we could
Though harm should come of it; so built the screen
You had begun, and gave them back their shade.
All this to prove we cared. Why is there then
No more to tell? We turned to other things.
I haven't any memory—have you?—
Of ever coming to the place again
To see if the birds lived the first night through,
And so at last to learn to use their wings.

22

"OUT, OUT—"

The buzz-saw snarled and rattled in the yard
And made dust and dropped stove-length sticks of wood,
Sweet-scented stuff when the breeze drew across it.
And from there those that lifted eyes could count
Five mountain ranges one behind the other
Under the sunset far into Vermont.
And the saw snarled and rattled, snarled and rattled,
As it ran light, or had to bear a load.
And nothing happened: day was all but done.
Call it a day, I wish they might have said
To please the boy by giving him the half hour
That a boy counts so much when saved from work.
His sister stood beside them in her apron

To tell them "Supper." At the word, the saw,
As if to prove saws knew what supper meant,
Leaped out at the boy's hand, or seemed to leap—
He must have given the hand. However it was,
Neither refused the meeting. But the hand!
The boy's first outcry was a rueful laugh,
As he swung toward them holding up the hand
Half in appeal, but half as if to keep
The life from spilling. Then the boy saw all—
Since he was old enough to know, big boy
Doing a man's work, though a child at heart—
He saw all spoiled. "Don't let him cut my hand off—
The doctor, when he comes. Don't let him, sister!"
So. But the hand was gone already.
The doctor put him in the dark of ether.
He lay and puffed his lips out with his breath.
And then—the watcher at his pulse took fright.
No one believed. They listened at his heart.
Little—less—nothing!—and that ended it.
No more to build on there. And they, since they
Were not the one dead, turned to their affairs.

23

BROWN'S DESCENT

OR THE WILLY-NILLY SLIDE

Brown lived at such a lofty farm
That everyone for miles could see
His lantern when he did his chores
In winter after half-past three.

And many must have seen him make
His wild descent from there one night,
'Cross lots, 'cross walls, 'cross everything,
Describing rings of lantern light.

Between the house and barn the gale
Got him by something he had on
And blew him out on the icy crust
That cased the world, and he was gone!

Walls were all buried, trees were few:
He saw no stay unless he stove
A hole in somewhere with his heel.
But though repeatedly he strove

And stamped and said things to himself,
And sometimes something seemed to yield,
He gained no foothold, but pursued
His journey down from field to field.

Sometimes he came with arms outspread

Like wings, revolving in the scene
Upon his longer axis, and
With no small dignity of mien.

Faster or slower as he chanced,
Sitting or standing as he chose,
According as he feared to risk
His neck, or thought to spare his clothes,

He never let the lantern drop.
And some exclaimed who saw afar
The figures he described with it,
"I wonder what those signals are

Brown makes at such an hour of night!
He's celebrating something strange.
I wonder if he's sold his farm,
Or been made Master of the Grange."

He reeled, he lurched, he bobbed, he checked;
He fell and made the lantern rattle
(But saved the light from going out.)
So half-way down he fought the battle

Incredulous of his own bad luck.
And then becoming reconciled
To everything, he gave it up
And came down like a coasting child.

"Well—I—be—" that was all he said,
As standing in the river road,
He looked back up the slippery slope

(Two miles it was) to his abode.

Sometimes as an authority
On motor-cars, I'm asked if I
Should say our stock was petered out,
And this is my sincere reply:

Yankees are what they always were.
Don't think Brown ever gave up hope
Of getting home again because
He couldn't climb that slippery slope;

Or even thought of standing there
Until the January thaw
Should take the polish off the crust.
He bowed with grace to natural law,

And then went round it on his feet,
After the manner of our stock;
Not much concerned for those to whom,
At that particular time o'clock,

It must have looked as if the course
He steered was really straight away
From that which he was headed for—
Not much concerned for them, I say;

No more so than became a man—
And politician at odd seasons.
I've kept Brown standing in the cold
While I invested him with reasons;

But now he snapped his eyes three times;

Then shook his lantern, saying, "Ile's
'Bout out!" and took the long way home
By road, a matter of several miles.

24

THE GUM-GATHERER

There overtook me and drew me in
  To his down-hill, early-morning stride,
  And set me five miles on my road
  Better than if he had had me ride,
  A man with a swinging bag for load
  And half the bag wound round his hand.
  We talked like barking above the din
  Of water we walked along beside.
  And for my telling him where I'd been
  And where I lived in mountain land
  To be coming home the way I was,
  He told me a little about himself.
  He came from higher up in the pass
  Where the grist of the new-beginning brooks
  Is blocks split off the mountain mass—
  And hopeless grist enough it looks
  Ever to grind to soil for grass.
  (The way it is will do for moss.)
  There he had built his stolen shack.
  It had to be a stolen shack
  Because of the fears of fire and loss
  That trouble the sleep of lumber folk:
  Visions of half the world burned black

And the sun shrunken yellow in smoke.
We know who when they come to town
Bring berries under the wagon seat,
Or a basket of eggs between their feet;
What this man brought in a cotton sack
Was gum, the gum of the mountain spruce.
He showed me lumps of the scented stuff
Like uncut jewels, dull and rough.
It comes to market golden brown;
But turns to pink between the teeth.

I told him this is a pleasant life
To set your breast to the bark of trees
That all your days are dim beneath,
And reaching up with a little knife,
To loose the resin and take it down
And bring it to market when you please.

25

THE LINE-GANG

Here come the line-gang pioneering by.
    They throw a forest down less cut than broken.
    They plant dead trees for living, and the dead
    They string together with a living thread.
    They string an instrument against the sky
    Wherein words whether beaten out or spoken
    Will run as hushed as when they were a thought.
    But in no hush they string it: they go past
    With shouts afar to pull the cable taut,

49

To hold it hard until they make it fast,
To ease away–they have it. With a laugh,
An oath of towns that set the wild at naught
They bring the telephone and telegraph.

26

THE VANISHING RED

He is said to have been the last Red Man
    In Acton. And the Miller is said to have laughed–
    If you like to call such a sound a laugh.
    But he gave no one else a laugher's license.
    For he turned suddenly grave as if to say,
    "Whose business,–if I take it on myself,
    Whose business–but why talk round the barn?–
    When it's just that I hold with getting a thing done with."
    You can't get back and see it as he saw it.
    It's too long a story to go into now.
    You'd have to have been there and lived it.
    Then you wouldn't have looked on it as just a matter
    Of who began it between the two races.

    Some guttural exclamation of surprise
    The Red Man gave in poking about the mill
    Over the great big thumping shuffling mill-stone
    Disgusted the Miller physically as coming
    From one who had no right to be heard from.
    "Come, John," he said, "you want to see the wheel pit?"

    He took him down below a cramping rafter,

And showed him, through a manhole in the floor,
The water in desperate straits like frantic fish,
Salmon and sturgeon, lashing with their tails.
Then he shut down the trap door with a ring in it
That jangled even above the general noise,
And came up stairs alone—and gave that laugh,
And said something to a man with a meal-sack
That the man with the meal-sack didn't catch—then.
Oh, yes, he showed John the wheel pit all right.

27

SNOW

The three stood listening to a fresh access
   Of wind that caught against the house a moment,
   Gulped snow, and then blew free again—the Coles
   Dressed, but dishevelled from some hours of sleep,
   Meserve belittled in the great skin coat he wore.

   Meserve was first to speak. He pointed backward
   Over his shoulder with his pipe-stem, saying,
   "You can just see it glancing off the roof
   Making a great scroll upward toward the sky,
   Long enough for recording all our names on.—
   I think I'll just call up my wife and tell her
   I'm here—so far—and starting on again.
   I'll call her softly so that if she's wise
   And gone to sleep, she needn't wake to answer."
   Three times he barely stirred the bell, then listened.
   "Why, Lett, still up? Lett, I'm at Cole's. I'm late.

I called you up to say Good-night from here
Before I went to say Good-morning there.–
I thought I would.–I know, but, Lett–I know–
I could, but what's the sense? The rest won't be
So bad.–Give me an hour for it.–Ho, ho,
Three hours to here! But that was all up hill;
The rest is down.–Why no, no, not a wallow:
They kept their heads and took their time to it
Like darlings, both of them. They're in the barn.–
My dear, I'm coming just the same. I didn't
Call you to ask you to invite me home.–"
He lingered for some word she wouldn't say,
Said it at last himself, "Good-night," and then,
Getting no answer, closed the telephone.
The three stood in the lamplight round the table
With lowered eyes a moment till he said,
"I'll just see how the horses are."

"Yes, do,"

Both the Coles said together. Mrs. Cole
Added: "You can judge better after seeing.–
I want you here with me, Fred. Leave him here,
Brother Meserve. You know to find your way
Out through the shed."

"I guess I know my way,

I guess I know where I can find my name
Carved in the shed to tell me who I am
If it don't tell me where I am. I used
To play–"

"You tend your horses and come back.

Fred Cole, you're going to let him!"

"Well, aren't you?

How can you help yourself?"

"I called him Brother.

Why did I call him that?"

"It's right enough.

That's all you ever heard him called round here.
He seems to have lost off his Christian name."

"Christian enough I should call that myself.
He took no notice, did he? Well, at least
I didn't use it out of love of him,
The dear knows. I detest the thought of him
With his ten children under ten years old.
I hate his wretched little Racker Sect,
All's ever I heard of it, which isn't much.
But that's not saying–Look, Fred Cole, it's twelve,
Isn't it, now? He's been here half an hour.
He says he left the village store at nine.
Three hours to do four miles–a mile an hour
Or not much better. Why, it doesn't seem
As if a man could move that slow and move.
Try to think what he did with all that time.
And three miles more to go!"

"Don't let him go.

Stick to him, Helen. Make him answer you.
That sort of man talks straight on all his life
From the last thing he said himself, stone deaf
To anything anyone else may say.
I should have thought, though, you could make him hear
you."

"What is he doing out a night like this?
Why can't he stay at home?"

"He had to preach."

"It's no night to be out."

"He may be small,

He may be good, but one thing's sure, he's tough."

"And strong of stale tobacco."

"He'll pull through."

"You only say so. Not another house
Or shelter to put into from this place
To theirs. I'm going to call his wife again."

"Wait and he may. Let's see what he will do.
Let's see if he will think of her again.
But then I doubt he's thinking of himself
He doesn't look on it as anything."

"He shan't go—there!"

"It *is* a night, my dear."

"One thing: he didn't drag God into it."

"He don't consider it a case for God."

"You think so, do you? You don't know the kind.
He's getting up a miracle this minute.
Privately—to himself, right now, he's thinking
He'll make a case of it if he succeeds,
But keep still if he fails."

"Keep still all over.

He'll be dead—dead and buried."

"Such a trouble!

Not but I've every reason not to care
What happens to him if it only takes
Some of the sanctimonious conceit
Out of one of those pious scalawags."

"Nonsense to that! You want to see him safe."

"You like the runt."

"Don't you a little?"

"Well,

I don't like what he's doing, which is what
You like, and like him for."

"Oh, yes you do.

You like your fun as well as anyone;
Only you women have to put these airs on
To impress men. You've got us so ashamed
Of being men we can't look at a good fight
Between two boys and not feel bound to stop it.
Let the man freeze an ear or two, I say.–
He's here. I leave him all to you. Go in
And save his life.–All right, come in, Meserve.
Sit down, sit down. How did you find the horses?"

"Fine, fine."

"And ready for some more? My wife here

Says it won't do. You've got to give it up."

"Won't you to please me? Please! If I say please?
Mr. Meserve, I'll leave it to *your* wife.
What *did* your wife say on the telephone?"

Meserve seemed to heed nothing but the lamp
Or something not far from it on the table.
By straightening out and lifting a forefinger,
He pointed with his hand from where it lay
Like a white crumpled spider on his knee:
"That leaf there in your open book! It moved
Just then, I thought. It's stood erect like that,
There on the table, ever since I came,

Trying to turn itself backward or forward,
I've had my eye on it to make out which;
If forward, then it's with a friend's impatience—
You see I know—to get you on to things
It wants to see how you will take, if backward
It's from regret for something you have passed
And failed to see the good of. Never mind,
Things must expect to come in front of us
A many times—I don't say just how many—
That varies with the things—before we see them.
One of the lies would make it out that nothing
Ever presents itself before us twice.
Where would we be at last if that were so?
Our very life depends on everything's
Recurring till we answer from within.
The thousandth time may prove the charm.—That leaf!
It can't turn either way. It needs the wind's help.
But the wind didn't move it if it moved.
It moved itself. The wind's at naught in here.
It couldn't stir so sensitively poised
A thing as that. It couldn't reach the lamp
To get a puff of black smoke from the flame,
Or blow a rumple in the collie's coat.
You make a little foursquare block of air,
Quiet and light and warm, in spite of all
The illimitable dark and cold and storm,
And by so doing give these three, lamp, dog,
And book-leaf, that keep near you, their repose;
Though for all anyone can tell, repose
May be the thing you haven't, yet you give it.
So false it is that what we haven't we can't give;
So false, that what we always say is true.
I'll have to turn the leaf if no one else will.

It won't lie down. Then let it stand. Who cares?"

"I shouldn't want to hurry you, Meserve,
But if you're going—Say you'll stay, you know?
But let me raise this curtain on a scene,
And show you how it's piling up against you.
You see the snow-white through the white of frost?
Ask Helen how far up the sash it's climbed
Since last we read the gage."

"It looks as if

Some pallid thing had squashed its features flat
And its eyes shut with overeagerness
To see what people found so interesting
In one another, and had gone to sleep
Of its own stupid lack of understanding,
Or broken its white neck of mushroom stuff
Short off, and died against the window-pane."

"Brother Meserve, take care, you'll scare yourself
More than you will us with such nightmare talk.
It's you it matters to, because it's you
Who have to go out into it alone."

"Let him talk, Helen, and perhaps he'll stay."

"Before you drop the curtain—I'm reminded:
You recollect the boy who came out here
To breathe the air one winter—had a room
Down at the Averys'? Well, one sunny morning
After a downy storm, he passed our place
And found me banking up the house with snow.

And I was burrowing in deep for warmth,
Piling it well above the window-sills.
The snow against the window caught his eye.
'Hey, that's a pretty thought'–those were his words.
'So you can think it's six feet deep outside,
While you sit warm and read up balanced rations.
You can't get too much winter in the winter.'
Those were his words. And he went home and all
But banked the daylight out of Avery's windows.
Now you and I would go to no such length.
At the same time you can't deny it makes
It not a mite worse, sitting here, we three,
Playing our fancy, to have the snowline run
So high across the pane outside. There where
There is a sort of tunnel in the frost
More like a tunnel than a hole–way down
At the far end of it you see a stir
And quiver like the frayed edge of the drift
Blown in the wind. I *like* that–I like *that*.
Well, now I leave you, people."

"Come, Meserve,

We thought you were deciding not to go–
The ways you found to say the praise of comfort
And being where you are. You want to stay."

"I'll own it's cold for such a fall of snow.
This house is frozen brittle, all except
This room you sit in. If you think the wind
Sounds further off, it's not because it's dying;
You're further under in the snow–that's all–
And feel it less. Hear the soft bombs of dust

It bursts against us at the chimney mouth,
And at the eaves. I like it from inside
More than I shall out in it. But the horses
Are rested and it's time to say good-night,
And let you get to bed again. Good-night,
Sorry I had to break in on your sleep."

"Lucky for you you did. Lucky for you
You had us for a half-way station
To stop at. If you were the kind of man
Paid heed to women, you'd take my advice
And for your family's sake stay where you are.
But what good is my saying it over and over?
You've done more than you had a right to think
You could do—*now*. You know the risk you take
In going on."

"Our snow-storms as a rule

Aren't looked on as man-killers, and although
I'd rather be the beast that sleeps the sleep
Under it all, his door sealed up and lost,
Than the man fighting it to keep above it,
Yet think of the small birds at roost and not
In nests. Shall I be counted less than they are?
Their bulk in water would be frozen rock
In no time out to-night. And yet to-morrow
They will come budding boughs from tree to tree
Flirting their wings and saying Chickadee,
As if not knowing what you meant by the word storm."

"But why when no one wants you to go on?
Your wife—she doesn't want you to. We don't,

And you yourself don't want to. Who else is there?"

"Save us from being cornered by a woman.
Well, there's"–She told Fred afterward that in
The pause right there, she thought the dreaded word
Was coming, "God." But no, he only said
"Well, there's–the storm. That says I must go on.
That wants me as a war might if it came.
Ask any man."

He threw her that as something

To last her till he got outside the door.
He had Cole with him to the barn to see him off.
When Cole returned he found his wife still standing
Beside the table near the open book,
Not reading it.

"Well, what kind of a man

Do you call that?" she said.

"He had the gift

Of words, or is it tongues, I ought to say?"

"Was ever such a man for seeing likeness?"

"Or disregarding people's civil questions–
What? We've found out in one hour more about him
Than we had seeing him pass by in the road
A thousand times. If that's the way he preaches!
You didn't think you'd keep him after all.

Oh, I'm not blaming you. He didn't leave you
Much say in the matter, and I'm just as glad
We're not in for a night of him. No sleep
If he had stayed. The least thing set him going.
It's quiet as an empty church without him."

"But how much better off are we as it is?
We'll have to sit here till we know he's safe."

"Yes, I suppose you'll want to, but I shouldn't.
He knows what he can do, or he wouldn't try.
Get into bed I say, and get some rest.
He won't come back, and if he telephones,
It won't be for an hour or two."

"Well then.

We can't be any help by sitting here
And living his fight through with him, I suppose."

$$* \quad * \quad * \quad * \quad * \quad * \quad * \quad * \quad * \quad *$$

Cole had been telephoning in the dark.
Mrs. Cole's voice came from an inner room:
"Did she call you or you call her?"

"She me.

You'd better dress: you won't go back to bed.
We must have been asleep: it's three and after."

"Had she been ringing long? I'll get my wrapper.

I want to speak to her."

"All she said was,

He hadn't come and had he really started."

"She knew he had, poor thing, two hours ago."

"He had the shovel. He'll have made a fight."

"Why did I ever let him leave this house!"

"Don't begin that. You did the best you could
To keep him—though perhaps you didn't quite
Conceal a wish to see him show the spunk
To disobey you. Much his wife'll thank you."

"Fred, after all I said! You shan't make out
That it was any way but what it was.
Did she let on by any word she said
She didn't thank me?"

"When I told her 'Gone,'

'Well then,' she said, and 'Well then'—like a threat.
And then her voice came scraping slow: 'Oh, you,
Why did you let him go'?"

"Asked why we let him?

You let me there. I'll ask her why she let him.
She didn't dare to speak when he was here.
Their number's—twenty-one? The thing won't work.

Someone's receiver's down. The handle stumbles.
The stubborn thing, the way it jars your arm!
It's theirs. She's dropped it from her hand and gone."

"Try speaking. Say 'Hello'!"

"Hello. Hello."

"What do you hear?"

"I hear an empty room—

You know—it sounds that way. And yes, I hear—
I think I hear a clock—and windows rattling.
No step though. If she's there she's sitting down."

"Shout, she may hear you."

"Shouting is no good."

"Keep speaking then."

"Hello. Hello. Hello.

You don't suppose—? She wouldn't go out doors?"

"I'm half afraid that's just what she might do."

"And leave the children?"

"Wait and call again.

You can't hear whether she has left the door

Wide open and the wind's blown out the lamp
And the fire's died and the room's dark and cold?"

"One of two things, either she's gone to bed
Or gone out doors."

"In which case both are lost.

Do you know what she's like? Have you ever met her?
It's strange she doesn't want to speak to us."

"Fred, see if you can hear what I hear. Come."

"A clock maybe."

"Don't you hear something else?"

"Not talking."

"No."

"Why, yes, I hear—what is it?"

"What do you say it is?"

"A baby's crying!

Frantic it sounds, though muffled and far off."

"Its mother wouldn't let it cry like that,
Not if she's there."

"What do you make of it?"

"There's only one thing possible to make,
That is, assuming–that she has gone out.
Of course she hasn't though." They both sat down
Helpless. "There's nothing we can do till morning."

"Fred, I shan't let you think of going out."

"Hold on." The double bell began to chirp.
They started up. Fred took the telephone.
"Hello, Meserve. You're there, then!–And your wife?
Good! Why I asked–she didn't seem to answer.
He says she went to let him in the barn.–
We're glad. Oh, say no more about it, man.
Drop in and see us when you're passing."

"Well,

She has him then, though what she wants him for
I *don't* see."

"Possibly not for herself.

Maybe she only wants him for the children."

"The whole to-do seems to have been for nothing.
What spoiled our night was to him just his fun.
What did he come in for?–To talk and visit?
Thought he'd just call to tell us it was snowing.
If he thinks he is going to make our house
A halfway coffee house 'twixt town and nowhere––"

"I thought you'd feel you'd been too much concerned."

"You think you haven't been concerned yourself."

"If you mean he was inconsiderate
To rout us out to think for him at midnight
And then take our advice no more than nothing,
Why, I agree with you. But let's forgive him.
We've had a share in one night of his life.
What'll you bet he ever calls again?"

28

THE SOUND OF THE TREES

I wonder about the trees.
   Why do we wish to bear
   Forever the noise of these
   More than another noise
   So close to our dwelling place?
   We suffer them by the day
   Till we lose all measure of pace,
   And fixity in our joys,
   And acquire a listening air.
   They are that that talks of going
   But never gets away;
   And that talks no less for knowing,
   As it grows wiser and older,
   That now it means to stay.
   My feet tug at the floor
   And my head sways to my shoulder
   Sometimes when I watch trees sway,
   From the window or the door.
   I shall set forth for somewhere,
   I shall make the reckless choice
   Some day when they are in voice
   And tossing so as to scare
   The white clouds over them on.
   I shall have less to say,
   But I shall be gone.

*   *   *   *   *   *   *   *   *   *

Part III

A BOY'S WILL

1

INTO MY OWN

ONE of my wishes is that those dark trees,
    So old and firm they scarcely show the breeze,
    Were not, as 'twere, the merest mask of gloom,
    But stretched away unto the edge of doom.

    I should not be withheld but that some day
    Into their vastness I should steal away,
    Fearless of ever finding open land,
    Or highway where the slow wheel pours the sand.

    I do not see why I should e'er turn back,
    Or those should not set forth upon my track
    To overtake me, who should miss me here
    And long to know if still I held them dear.

    They would not find me changed from him they knew—
    Only more sure of all I thought was true.

2

GHOST HOUSE

I DWELL in a lonely house I know
    That vanished many a summer ago,
    And left no trace but the cellar walls,
    And a cellar in which the daylight falls,

And the purple-stemmed wild raspberries grow.

O'er ruined fences the grape-vines shield
The woods come back to the mowing field;
The orchard tree has grown one copse
Of new wood and old where the woodpecker chops;
The footpath down to the well is healed.

I dwell with a strangely aching heart
In that vanished abode there far apart
On that disused and forgotten road
That has no dust-bath now for the toad.
Night comes; the black bats tumble and dart;

The whippoorwill is coming to shout
And hush and cluck and flutter about:
I hear him begin far enough away
Full many a time to say his say
Before he arrives to say it out.

It is under the small, dim, summer star.
I know not who these mute folk are
Who share the unlit place with me–
Those stones out under the low-limbed tree
Doubtless bear names that the mosses mar.

They are tireless folk, but slow and sad,
Though two, close-keeping, are lass and lad,–
With none among them that ever sings,
And yet, in view of how many things,
As sweet companions as might be had.

3

MY NOVEMBER GUEST

MY Sorrow, when she's here with me,
  Thinks these dark days of autumn rain
  Are beautiful as days can be;
  She loves the bare, the withered tree;
  She walks the sodden pasture lane.

Her pleasure will not let me stay.
  She talks and I am fain to list:
  She's glad the birds are gone away,
  She's glad her simple worsted gray
  Is silver now with clinging mist.

The desolate, deserted trees,
  The faded earth, the heavy sky,
  The beauties she so truly sees,
  She thinks I have no eye for these,
  And vexes me for reason why.

Not yesterday I learned to know
  The love of bare November days
  Before the coming of the snow,
  But it were vain to tell her so,
  And they are better for her praise.

4

LOVE AND A QUESTION

A STRANGER came to the door at eve,
    And he spoke the bridegroom fair.
He bore a green-white stick in his hand,
    And, for all burden, care.
He asked with the eyes more than the lips
    For a shelter for the night,
And he turned and looked at the road afar
    Without a window light.

The bridegroom came forth into the porch
    With, 'Let us look at the sky,
And question what of the night to be,
    Stranger, you and I.'
The woodbine leaves littered the yard,
    The woodbine berries were blue,
Autumn, yes, winter was in the wind;
    'Stranger, I wish I knew.'

Within, the bride in the dusk alone
    Bent over the open fire,
Her face rose-red with the glowing coal
    And the thought of the heart's desire.

The bridegroom looked at the weary road,
    Yet saw but her within,
And wished her heart in a case of gold

And pinned with a silver pin.

The bridegroom thought it little to give
A dole of bread, a purse,
A heartfelt prayer for the poor of God,
Or for the rich a curse;

But whether or not a man was asked
To mar the love of two
By harboring woe in the bridal house,
The bridegroom wished he knew.

5

A LATE WALK

WHEN I go up through the mowing field,
  The headless aftermath,
  Smooth-laid like thatch with the heavy dew,
  Half closes the garden path.

And when I come to the garden ground,
  The whir of sober birds
  Up from the tangle of withered weeds
  Is sadder than any words.

A tree beside the wall stands bare,
  But a leaf that lingered brown,
  Disturbed, I doubt not, by my thought,
  Comes softly rattling down.

I end not far from my going forth
By picking the faded blue
Of the last remaining aster flower
To carry again to you.

6

STARS

HOW countlessly they congregate
   O'er our tumultuous snow,
   Which flows in shapes as tall as trees
   When wintry winds do blow!–

As if with keenness for our fate,
   Our faltering few steps on
   To white rest, and a place of rest
   Invisible at dawn,–

And yet with neither love nor hate,
   Those stars like some snow-white
   Minerva's snow-white marble eyes
   Without the gift of sight.

7

STORM FEAR

WHEN the wind works against us in the dark,
    And pelts with snow
    The lowest chamber window on the east,
    And whispers with a sort of stifled bark,
    The beast,
    'Come out! Come out!'–
It costs no inward struggle not to go,
    Ah, no!
I count our strength,
    Two and a child,
Those of us not asleep subdued to mark
How the cold creeps as the fire dies at length,–
    How drifts are piled,
Dooryard and road ungraded,
Till even the comforting barn grows far away
    And my heart owns a doubt
Whether 'tis in us to arise with day
    And save ourselves unaided.

8

WIND AND WINDOW FLOWER

LOVERS, forget your love,
    And list to the love of these,
    She a window flower,

And he a winter breeze.

When the frosty window veil
Was melted down at noon,
And the cagèd yellow bird
Hung over her in tune,

He marked her through the pane,
He could not help but mark,
And only passed her by,
To come again at dark.

He was a winter wind,
Concerned with ice and snow,
Dead weeds and unmated birds,
And little of love could know.

But he sighed upon the sill,
He gave the sash a shake,
As witness all within
Who lay that night awake.

Perchance he half prevailed
To win her for the flight
From the firelit looking-glass
And warm stove-window light.

But the flower leaned aside
And thought of naught to say,
And morning found the breeze
A hundred miles away.

9

TO THE THAWING WIND

COME with rain, O loud Southwester!
  Bring the singer, bring the nester;
  Give the buried flower a dream;
  Make the settled snow-bank steam;
  Find the brown beneath the white;
  But whate'er you do to-night,
  Bathe my window, make it flow,
  Melt it as the ices go;
  Melt the glass and leave the sticks
  Like a hermit's crucifix;
  Burst into my narrow stall;
  Swing the picture on the wall;
  Run the rattling pages o'er;
  Scatter poems on the floor;
  Turn the poet out of door.

10

A PRAYER IN SPRING

OH, give us pleasure in the flowers to-day;
  And give us not to think so far away
  As the uncertain harvest; keep us here
  All simply in the springing of the year.

  Oh, give us pleasure in the orchard white,

Like nothing else by day, like ghosts by night;
And make us happy in the happy bees,
The swarm dilating round the perfect trees.

And make us happy in the darting bird
That suddenly above the bees is heard,
The meteor that thrusts in with needle bill,
And off a blossom in mid air stands still.

For this is love and nothing else is love,
The which it is reserved for God above
To sanctify to what far ends He will,
But which it only needs that we fulfil.

11

FLOWER-GATHERING

I LEFT you in the morning,
    And in the morning glow,
    You walked a way beside me
    To make me sad to go.
    Do you know me in the gloaming,
    Gaunt and dusty grey with roaming?
    Are you dumb because you know me not,
    Or dumb because you know?

    All for me? And not a question
    For the faded flowers gay
    That could take me from beside you
    For the ages of a day?

They are yours, and be the measure
Of their worth for you to treasure,
The measure of the little while
That I've been long away.

12

ROSE POGONIAS

A SATURATED meadow,
  Sun-shaped and jewel-small,
  A circle scarcely wider
  Than the trees around were tall;
  Where winds were quite excluded,
  And the air was stifling sweet
  With the breath of many flowers,–
  A temple of the heat.

  There we bowed us in the burning,
  As the sun's right worship is,
  To pick where none could miss them
  A thousand orchises;
  For though the grass was scattered,
  Yet every second spear
  Seemed tipped with wings of color,
  That tinged the atmosphere.

  We raised a simple prayer
  Before we left the spot,
  That in the general mowing
  That place might be forgot;

Or if not all so favoured,
Obtain such grace of hours,
That none should mow the grass there
While so confused with flowers.

13

ASKING FOR ROSES

A HOUSE that lacks, seemingly, mistress and master,
    With doors that none but the wind ever closes,
    Its floor all littered with glass and with plaster;
    It stands in a garden of old-fashioned roses.

I pass by that way in the gloaming with Mary;
    'I wonder,' I say, 'who the owner of those is.
    'Oh, no one you know,' she answers me airy,
    'But one we must ask if we want any roses.'

So we must join hands in the dew coming coldly
    There in the hush of the wood that reposes,
    And turn and go up to the open door boldly,
    And knock to the echoes as beggars for roses.
'Pray, are you within there, Mistress Who-were-you?'
    'Tis Mary that speaks and our errand discloses.
'Pray, are you within there? Bestir you, bestir you!
    'Tis summer again; there's two come for roses.

'A word with you, that of the singer recalling—
    Old Herrick: a saying that every maid knows is
    A flower unplucked is but left to the falling,

And nothing is gained by not gathering roses.'

We do not loosen our hands' intertwining
(Not caring so very much what she supposes),
There when she comes on us mistily shining
And grants us by silence the boon of her roses.

14

WAITING

Afield at Dusk

WHAT things for dream there are when spectre-like,
Moving among tall haycocks lightly piled,
I enter alone upon the stubble field,
From which the laborers' voices late have died,
And in the antiphony of afterglow
And rising full moon, sit me down
Upon the full moon's side of the first haycock
And lose myself amid so many alike.

I dream upon the opposing lights of the hour,
Preventing shadow until the moon prevail;
I dream upon the night-hawks peopling heaven,
Each circling each with vague unearthly cry,
Or plunging headlong with fierce twang afar;
And on the bat's mute antics, who would seem
Dimly to have made out my secret place,
Only to lose it when he pirouettes,
And seek it endlessly with purblind haste;
On the last swallow's sweep; and on the rasp

In the abyss of odor and rustle at my back,
That, silenced by my advent, finds once more,
After an interval, his instrument,
And tries once—twice—and thrice if I be there;
And on the worn book of old-golden song
I brought not here to read, it seems, but hold
And freshen in this air of withering sweetness;
But on the memory of one absent most,
For whom these lines when they shall greet her eye.

15

IN A VALE

WHEN I was young, we dwelt in a vale
    By a misty fen that rang all night,
    And thus it was the maidens pale
    I knew so well, whose garments trail
    Across the reeds to a window light.

    The fen had every kind of bloom,
    And for every kind there was a face,
    And a voice that has sounded in my room
    Across the sill from the outer gloom.
    Each came singly unto her place,

    But all came every night with the mist;
    And often they brought so much to say
    Of things of moment to which, they wist,
    One so lonely was fain to list,

That the stars were almost faded away

Before the last went, heavy with dew,
Back to the place from which she came—
Where the bird was before it flew,
Where the flower was before it grew,
Where bird and flower were one and the same.

And thus it is I know so well
Why the flower has odor, the bird has song.
You have only to ask me, and I can tell.
No, not vainly there did I dwell,
Nor vainly listen all the night long.

16

A DREAM PANG

I HAD withdrawn in forest, and my song
    Was swallowed up in leaves that blew alway;
    And to the forest edge you came one day
(This was my dream) and looked and pondered long,
But did not enter, though the wish was strong:
    You shook your pensive head as who should say,
    'I dare not—too far in his footsteps stray—
He must seek me would he undo the wrong.

Not far, but near, I stood and saw it all
    Behind low boughs the trees let down outside;
    And the sweet pang it cost me not to call
And tell you that I saw does still abide.

But 'tis not true that thus I dwelt aloof,
For the wood wakes, and you are here for proof.

17

IN NEGLECT

THEY leave us so to the way we took,
  As two in whom they were proved mistaken,
  That we sit sometimes in the wayside nook,
  With mischievous, vagrant, seraphic look,
  And try if we cannot feel forsaken.

18

THE VANTAGE POINT

IF tired of trees I seek again mankind,
  Well I know where to hie me—in the dawn,
  To a slope where the cattle keep the lawn.
  There amid lolling juniper reclined,
  Myself unseen, I see in white defined
  Far off the homes of men, and farther still,
  The graves of men on an opposing hill,
  Living or dead, whichever are to mind.

And if by moon I have too much of these,
  I have but to turn on my arm, and lo,
  The sun-burned hillside sets my face aglow,

My breathing shakes the bluet like a breeze,
I smell the earth, I smell the bruisèd plant,
I look into the crater of the ant.

19

MOWING

THERE was never a sound beside the wood but one,
  And that was my long scythe whispering to the ground.
  What was it it whispered? I knew not well myself;
  Perhaps it was something about the heat of the sun,
  Something, perhaps, about the lack of sound–
  And that was why it whispered and did not speak.
  It was no dream of the gift of idle hours,
  Or easy gold at the hand of fay or elf:
  Anything more than the truth would have seemed too
weak
  To the earnest love that laid the swale in rows,
  Not without feeble-pointed spikes of flowers
  (Pale orchises), and scared a bright green snake.
  The fact is the sweetest dream that labor knows.
  My long scythe whispered and left the hay to make.

20

GOING FOR WATER

THE well was dry beside the door,
   And so we went with pail and can
   Across the fields behind the house
   To seek the brook if still it ran;

Not loth to have excuse to go,
   Because the autumn eve was fair
   (Though chill), because the fields were ours,
   And by the brook our woods were there.

We ran as if to meet the moon
   That slowly dawned behind the trees,
   The barren boughs without the leaves,
   Without the birds, without the breeze.

But once within the wood, we paused
   Like gnomes that hid us from the moon,
   Ready to run to hiding new
   With laughter when she found us soon.

Each laid on other a staying hand
   To listen ere we dared to look,
   And in the hush we joined to make
   We heard, we knew we heard the brook.

A note as from a single place,
   A slender tinkling fall that made

Now drops that floated on the pool
Like pearls, and now a silver blade.

21

REVELATION

WE make ourselves a place apart
　　Behind light words that tease and flout,
　　But oh, the agitated heart
　　Till someone find us really out.

　　'Tis pity if the case require
　　(Or so we say) that in the end
　　We speak the literal to inspire
　　The understanding of a friend.

　　But so with all, from babes that play
　　At hide-and-seek to God afar,
　　So all who hide too well away
　　Must speak and tell us where they are.

22

THE TRIAL BY EXISTENCE

EVEN the bravest that are slain
　　Shall not dissemble their surprise
　　On waking to find valor reign,

Even as on earth, in paradise;
And where they sought without the sword
Wide fields of asphodel fore'er,
To find that the utmost reward
Of daring should be still to dare.

The light of heaven falls whole and white
And is not shattered into dyes,
The light for ever is morning light;
The hills are verdured pasture-wise;
The angel hosts with freshness go,
And seek with laughter what to brave;–
And binding all is the hushed snow
Of the far-distant breaking wave.

And from a cliff-top is proclaimed
The gathering of the souls for birth,
The trial by existence named,
The obscuration upon earth.
And the slant spirits trooping by
In streams and cross- and counter-streams
Can but give ear to that sweet cry
For its suggestion of what dreams!

And the more loitering are turned
To view once more the sacrifice
Of those who for some good discerned
Will gladly give up paradise.
And a white shimmering concourse rolls
Toward the throne to witness there
The speeding of devoted souls
Which God makes his especial care.

And none are taken but who will,
Having first heard the life read out
That opens earthward, good and ill,
Beyond the shadow of a doubt;
And very beautifully God limns,
And tenderly, life's little dream,
But naught extenuates or dims,
Setting the thing that is supreme.

Nor is there wanting in the press
Some spirit to stand simply forth,
Heroic in its nakedness,
Against the uttermost of earth.
The tale of earth's unhonored things
Sounds nobler there than 'neath the sun;
And the mind whirls and the heart sings,
And a shout greets the daring one.

But always God speaks at the end:
'One thought in agony of strife
The bravest would have by for friend,
The memory that he chose the life;
But the pure fate to which you go
Admits no memory of choice,
Or the woe were not earthly woe
To which you give the assenting voice.'

And so the choice must be again,
But the last choice is still the same;
And the awe passes wonder then,
And a hush falls for all acclaim.
And God has taken a flower of gold
And broken it, and used therefrom

The mystic link to bind and hold
Spirit to matter till death come.

'Tis of the essence of life here,
Though we choose greatly, still to lack
The lasting memory at all clear,
That life has for us on the wrack
Nothing but what we somehow chose;
Thus are we wholly stripped of pride
In the pain that has but one close,
Bearing it crushed and mystified.

23

IN EQUAL SACRIFICE

THUS of old the Douglas did:
He left his land as he was bid
With the royal heart of Robert the Bruce
In a golden case with a golden lid,

To carry the same to the Holy Land;
By which we see and understand
That that was the place to carry a heart
At loyalty and love's command,

And that was the case to carry it in.
The Douglas had not far to win
Before he came to the land of Spain,
Where long a holy war had been

Against the too-victorious Moor;
And there his courage could not endure
Not to strike a blow for God
Before he made his errand sure.

And ever it was intended so,
That a man for God should strike a blow,
No matter the heart he has in charge
For the Holy Land where hearts should go.

But when in battle the foe were met,
The Douglas found him sore beset,
With only strength of the fighting arm
For one more battle passage yet–

And that as vain to save the day
As bring his body safe away–
Only a signal deed to do
And a last sounding word to say.

The heart he wore in a golden chain
He swung and flung forth into the plain,
And followed it crying 'Heart or death!'
And fighting over it perished fain.

So may another do of right,
Give a heart to the hopeless fight,
The more of right the more he loves;
So may another redouble might

For a few swift gleams of the angry brand,
Scorning greatly not to demand
In equal sacrifice with his

The heart he bore to the Holy Land.

24

THE TUFT OF FLOWERS

I WENT to turn the grass once after one
Who mowed it in the dew before the sun.

The dew was gone that made his blade so keen
Before I came to view the leveled scene.

I looked for him behind an isle of trees;
I listened for his whetstone on the breeze.

But he had gone his way, the grass all mown,
And I must be, as he had been,–alone,

'As all must be,' I said within my heart,
'Whether they work together or apart.'

But as I said it, swift there passed me by
On noiseless wing a 'wildered butterfly,

Seeking with memories grown dim o'er night
Some resting flower of yesterday's delight.

And once I marked his flight go round and round,
As where some flower lay withering on the ground.

And then he flew as far as eye could see,

And then on tremulous wing came back to me.

I thought of questions that have no reply,
And would have turned to toss the grass to dry;

But he turned first, and led my eye to look
At a tall tuft of flowers beside a brook,

A leaping tongue of bloom the scythe had spared
Beside a reedy brook the scythe had bared.

I left my place to know them by their name,
Finding them butterfly weed when I came.

The mower in the dew had loved them thus,
By leaving them to flourish, not for us,

Nor yet to draw one thought of ours to him.
But from sheer morning gladness at the brim.

The butterfly and I had lit upon,
Nevertheless, a message from the dawn,

That made me hear the wakening birds around,
And hear his long scythe whispering to the ground,

And feel a spirit kindred to my own;
So that henceforth I worked no more alone;

But glad with him, I worked as with his aid,
And weary, sought at noon with him the shade;

And dreaming, as it were, held brotherly speech

With one whose thought I had not hoped to reach.

'Men work together,' I told him from the heart,
'Whether they work together or apart.'

25

SPOILS OF THE DEAD

TWO fairies it was
   On a still summer day
   Came forth in the woods
   With the flowers to play.

   The flowers they plucked
   They cast on the ground
   For others, and those
   For still others they found.

   Flower-guided it was
   That they came as they ran
   On something that lay
   In the shape of a man.

   The snow must have made
   The feathery bed
   When this one fell
   On the sleep of the dead.

   But the snow was gone
   A long time ago,

And the body he wore
Nigh gone with the snow.

The fairies drew near
And keenly espied
A ring on his hand
And a chain at his side.

They knelt in the leaves
And eerily played
With the glittering things,
And were not afraid.

And when they went home
To hide in their burrow,
They took them along
To play with to-morrow.

When you came on death,
Did you not come flower-guided
Like the elves in the wood?
I remember that I did.

But I recognised death
With sorrow and dread,
And I hated and hate
The spoils of the dead.

26

PAN WITH US

PAN came out of the woods one day,–
    His skin and his hair and his eyes were gray,
    The gray of the moss of walls were they,–
    And stood in the sun and looked his fill
    At wooded valley and wooded hill.

    He stood in the zephyr, pipes in hand,
    On a height of naked pasture land;
    In all the country he did command
    He saw no smoke and he saw no roof.
    That was well! and he stamped a hoof.

    His heart knew peace, for none came here
    To this lean feeding save once a year
    Someone to salt the half-wild steer,
    Or homespun children with clicking pails
    Who see no little they tell no tales.

    He tossed his pipes, too hard to teach
    A new-world song, far out of reach,
    For a sylvan sign that the blue jay's screech
    And the whimper of hawks beside the sun
    Were music enough for him, for one.

    Times were changed from what they were:
    Such pipes kept less of power to stir
    The fruited bough of the juniper

And the fragile bluets clustered there
Than the merest aimless breath of air.

They were pipes of pagan mirth,
And the world had found new terms of worth.
He laid him down on the sun-burned earth
And ravelled a flower and looked away–
Play? Play?–What should he play?

27

THE DEMIURGE'S LAUGH

IT was far in the sameness of the wood;
    I was running with joy on the Demon's trail,
    Though I knew what I hunted was no true god.
    It was just as the light was beginning to fail
    That I suddenly heard–all I needed to hear:
    It has lasted me many and many a year.

The sound was behind me instead of before,
    A sleepy sound, but mocking half,
    As of one who utterly couldn't care.
    The Demon arose from his wallow to laugh,
    Brushing the dirt from his eye as he went;
    And well I knew what the Demon meant.

I shall not forget how his laugh rang out.
    I felt as a fool to have been so caught,
    And checked my steps to make pretence
    It was something among the leaves I sought

(Though doubtful whether he stayed to see).
Thereafter I sat me against a tree.

28

NOW CLOSE THE WINDOWS

NOW close the windows and hush all the fields;
    If the trees must, let them silently toss;
    No bird is singing now, and if there is,
    Be it my loss.

It will be long ere the marshes resume,
    It will be long ere the earliest bird:
    So close the windows and not hear the wind,
    But see all wind-stirred.

29

A LINE-STORM SONG

THE line-storm clouds fly tattered and swift,
    The road is forlorn all day,
    Where a myriad snowy quartz stones lift,
    And the hoof-prints vanish away.
    The roadside flowers, too wet for the bee,
    Expend their bloom in vain.
    Come over the hills and far with me,

And be my love in the rain.

The birds have less to say for themselves
In the wood-world's torn despair
Than now these numberless years the elves,
Although they are no less there:
All song of the woods is crushed like some
Wild, easily shattered rose.
Come, be my love in the wet woods; come,
Where the boughs rain when it blows.

There is the gale to urge behind
And bruit our singing down,
And the shallow waters aflutter with wind
From which to gather your gown.
What matter if we go clear to the west,
And come not through dry-shod?
For wilding brooch shall wet your breast
The rain-fresh goldenrod.

Oh, never this whelming east wind swells
But it seems like the sea's return
To the ancient lands where it left the shells
Before the age of the fern;
And it seems like the time when after doubt
Our love came back amain.
Oh, come forth into the storm and rout
And be my love in the rain.

30

OCTOBER

O HUSHED October morning mild,
   Thy leaves have ripened to the fall;
   To-morrow's wind, if it be wild,
   Should waste them all.
   The crows above the forest call;
   To-morrow they may form and go.
   O hushed October morning mild,
   Begin the hours of this day slow,
   Make the day seem to us less brief.
   Hearts not averse to being beguiled,
   Beguile us in the way you know;
   Release one leaf at break of day;
   At noon release another leaf;
   One from our trees, one far away;
   Retard the sun with gentle mist;
   Enchant the land with amethyst.
   Slow, slow!
   For the grapes' sake, if they were all,
   Whose leaves already are burnt with frost,
   Whose clustered fruit must else be lost—
   For the grapes' sake along the wall.

31

MY BUTTERFLY

THINE emulous fond flowers are dead, too,
  And the daft sun-assaulter, he
  That frighted thee so oft, is fled or dead:
  Save only me
  (Nor is it sad to thee!)
  Save only me
  There is none left to mourn thee in the fields.

  The gray grass is not dappled with the snow;
  Its two banks have not shut upon the river;
  But it is long ago–
  It seems forever–
  Since first I saw thee glance,
  With all the dazzling other ones,
  In airy dalliance,
  Precipitate in love,
  Tossed, tangled, whirled and whirled above,
  Like a limp rose-wreath in a fairy dance.
  When that was, the soft mist
  Of my regret hung not on all the land,
  And I was glad for thee,
  And glad for me, I wist.

  Thou didst not know, who tottered, wandering on high,
  That fate had made thee for the pleasure of the wind,
  With those great careless wings,

Nor yet did I.

And there were other things:
It seemed God let thee flutter from his gentle clasp:
Then fearful he had let thee win
Too far beyond him to be gathered in,
Snatched thee, o'er eager, with ungentle grasp.

Ah! I remember me
How once conspiracy was rife
Against my life–
The languor of it and the dreaming fond;
Surging, the grasses dizzied me of thought,
The breeze three odors brought,
And a gem-flower waved in a wand!

Then when I was distraught
And could not speak,
Sidelong, full on my cheek,
What should that reckless zephyr fling
But the wild touch of thy dye-dusty wing!

I found that wing broken to-day!
For thou are dead, I said,
And the strange birds say.
I found it with the withered leaves
Under the eaves.

32

RELUCTANCE

OUT through the fields and the woods
    And over the walls I have wended;
    I have climbed the hills of view
    And looked at the world, and descended;
    I have come by the highway home,
    And lo, it is ended.

    The leaves are all dead on the ground,
    Save those that the oak is keeping
    To ravel them one by one
    And let them go scraping and creeping
    Out over the crusted snow,
    When others are sleeping.

    And the dead leaves lie huddled and still,
    No longer blown hither and thither;
    The last lone aster is gone;
    The flowers of the witch-hazel wither;
    The heart is still aching to seek,
    But the feet question 'Whither?'

    Ah, when to the heart of man
    Was it ever less than a treason
    To go with the drift of things,
    To yield with a grace to reason,
    And bow and accept and accept the end
    Of a love or a season?